Bärbel Thetmeyer writes stories about teddy bears, bunnies, rabbits and more. She started writing them back in the 90's; the first stories were meant to be as special Christmas presents for the family's children. However, they were so liked, that the stories were then published as print editions at BoD, and since the new media e-books appeared on the market, her books are now, also available on Kindle as e-books and on iTunes.

In 2012 she made the acquaintance of a wonderful English lady who became the editor for the first translation. So, Bärbel started what she called "my big translation adventure" and in December 2012 her first ever-English book was published at BoD. "Little Beaver's Secrets".

Her aim is to enrich the fantasy of her readers of all ages and to give them a little escape from today's world! Come and join in!

Last year she started to translate the bunny stories and the first three; "Bo Bunny Stories 1, 2 & 3" was published at BoD in 2015 and "Bo Bunny Stories 4, 5, 6 & 7" in 2019.

The publication of these reminiscences is a tribute to the man Dr Kevin Phillips, and his Alter Ego, the bear Toddy Furrington. They had 1000's of followers on social media, and would all have liked to say something… alas, many found it too hard to put into words.

German National Library Information

This publication is registered at the German
National Library;

ISBN 9783752643336

C 2020 Bärbel Thetmeyer

Herstellung und Verlag:

BoD – Books on Demand, Norderstedt

info@bod.de www.bod.de

This book is dedicated to my dear friends Debbie Cullen and Di Gorton as well as Mrs. Natalie Rizvi, the wonderful niece of Dr Kevin Phillips and the numerous friends all over the world.

Without your encouragement and helpful support, I could not have realised this compilation.

Thank you!

Bärbel Thetmeyer

Be More Toddy

'Memories'
compiled by Bärbel Thetmeyer

"I think I'm a jolly lucky elderly bear."

Toddy Furrington

Introduction
by Bärbel Thetmeyer

Dr Kevin Phillips, an extraordinary man, became the focus of 1000's of followers lives on social media, through his alter ego, Toddy Furrington, a gentle, steampunk bear. With his exceptional strength, kindness and caring humour, he brought warmth, love and hope to so many, becoming not only a much-loved character on social platforms, but as the man in real life too.

Nothing was ever too much trouble for him; he always went that extra mile to help and assist, displaying an incredible ability, it would seem, to be in more than one place at a time!

The effect he had on people's lives was so enormous, that his sudden and unexpected death, shocked a whole community of fellow bear & animal lovers, as well as friends and acquaintances; this book is just a tiny offering of some of the heartfelt memories shared by some of his friends, who would all want to...
Be More Toddy!

Some of Toddy's own posts[1] on Twitter and CanBeSocial (CBS) are found in between these memories.

---

[1] these show up like this: *"Toddy Furrington"*

13

This book that you now hold in your hands is the result of their efforts to bring honour to Dr Kevin and Toddy, and keep their memory alive! These memories reflect exactly what made this person, Dr Kevin Phillips, expressed through his alter ego Toddy Furrington, so unique.

Profits from the sale of this book will be donated to a Commemorative Fund for Dr Kevin's favourite, the "Bumblebee Conservation Trust", and for the planting of flowers at his graveside.

Zackary Rabbit (cbs): Toddy's farewell

Toddy has moved up to heaven

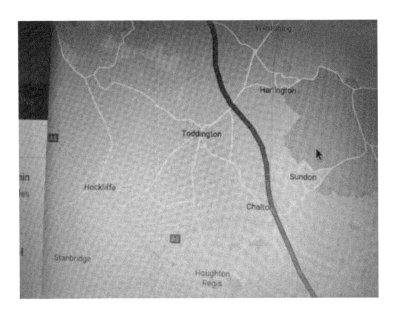

Notes on spelling and grammar

When communicating with Toddy Furrington, (the bear), on Twitter and CanBeSocial, many friends used a very special language. Some had even developed their own language. This made it very special.

All contributions are therefore, reproduced authentically.

So, it is not grammatical error you're reading in this book, everything is correct as spoken by Toddy's friends & followers.

Toddy would be amused and agree... with his famous chortle!

All special idioms are marked with a *.

All contributions are in alphabetical order.

This is a copy of Toddy's twitter account

Toddy Furrington
@ToddyFur

I'm a jolly steampunk bear enjoying cups of tea, jazz and gingery novels. Bee keeper at #FurryTails. Flying machine enthusiast in #TheAviators. TheAviators.Club
United Kingdom Joined March 2013

3,953 Following **7,135 Followers**

You didn't walk behind us;
I didn't want to lead.
You didn't walk in front of us;
You always walked beside us
being our friend.

Bärbel Thetmeyer

Archie's memories of Toddy & Kevin

by Archie's Girl, and @ArchieFuzzy and @TheHugHouse.

Kevin meant so much to me as he did all of us. As Olly he was one of my first Twitter friends. I sent Archie to visit him by post and he sent me many wonderful photos (that I am happy to share).

I left Twitter for a while, and when I came back I quickly was befriended by Toddy - although it was quite some time before I realized that Kevin was behind Olly AND Toddy. As Toddy's friend, I joined the #FurryTails team.

One of my favourite things to tell people about Kevin, is that from time to time I would ask him if he could make me a photo. I usually only had one particular photo in mind... But Kevin never did things half way. I'd soon get an email with 5 or 6 amazing photos in it.

A couple of years ago, Kevin asked me if he could send me a bear from his collection. He sent me a Dinker bear, a twecckle, and a poddlewink. He also sent me some chocolate and some packages of hot cocoa mix.... I had mentioned a time or two that I loved Chocolate Oranges, but I'd never had orange cocoa. He said he visited a few stores but was unsuccessful in finding chocolate orange cocoa mix. But he sent me some other flavours instead.

Kevin LOVED TBO bears, and from the minute I saw Ginger, I fell in love with them too. I bought a TBO bear named Colby, but when Kevin found out that I was saving up for a second one, he offered to buy it for me for Christmas. And that's how I got Tybearius Tiddler.

Somewhere along the way of sending me these things, I messaged and thanked him. His response is something that I will always cherish and something that I have shared with members of #ToddysHug. (see attached.) His words are something I have taken to heart as I know how much his bears and his Twitter family meant to him.

I'm sure I could go on and on. We had many conversations about Marvel movies and comics, Star Trek, Swing music, etc. I'm so grateful for our time together. But those are the important things.
With much love…

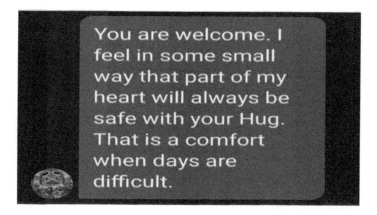

You are welcome. I feel in some small way that part of my heart will always be safe with your Hug. That is a comfort when days are difficult.

The Aviators on twitter

Some members of #The Aviators

Basil (Twitter) A Toast! by #TheAviators
@fluffybasil

Words to sum up Kevin & Toddy:
Kindhearted
Wise
Generous
Fun
Gracious
Adventurous
Organized
Clever
Welcoming
As we all say farewell & grieve in our own ways, let's
fondly remember fun & happy times shared

May we all endeavor to #bemoretoddy

General Biscuit @WestieBiscuit

He gave me my wings, and made
me smile every day. I will miss him

looks to the sky K9WBF signing
off, OVR.

Toddy taught us how to fly

Radar Asher

Rosie Amelia Bearhart

Sir Toddy Furrington

Gregory @belbaer

AVIATOR LICENSE

Name: @belbear

Aviator name: Victor Mike 99

Level: A. Aviator

Date: February 7th 2013   Signature @TheAviatorsClub:

Don't forget to put #TheAviators in your tweets!!!

This is meant for Anipals with a Twitter-account. It has nothing to do with flying in real life.

@TheAviatorsClub - - - #TheAviators

AVIATOR LICENSE

Name: @JezzerBear

Aviator name: Juliet Bravo India 658

Level: A. Aviator

Date: February 1st, 2014   Signature @TheAviatorsClub:

Don't forget to put #TheAviators in your tweets!!!

This is meant for Anipals with a Twitter-account. It has nothing to do with flying in real life.

Toddy's aviators' memories

I have had a smashing, (but very long) VIP day being shown around a Lancaster airplane and taxying up and down the runway. Wonderful experience for a small bear!

The airplane was amazing... and the sound of those four huge Merlin engines as we taxied up and down the runway was brilliant!

The Bear Family

by Burnie and Greg Bear @belbear and cbs

Two years ago, we sent this well-known poem to Toddy who admitted being deeply touched by the poetry.

I wandered lonely as a cloud

I wandered lonely as a cloud
That floats on high o'er vales and hills,
When all at once I saw a crowd,
A host, of golden daffodils;
Beside the lake, beneath the trees,
Fluttering and dancing in the breeze.

Continuous as the stars that shine
And twinkle on the milky way,
They stretched in never-ending line
Along the margin of a bay:
Ten thousand saw I at a glance,
Tossing their heads in sprightly dance.

The waves beside them danced; but they
Out-did the sparkling waves in glee:
A poet could not but be gay,
In such a jocund company:
I gazed – and gazed – but little thought
What wealth the show to me had brought:

For oft, when on my couch I lie
In vacant or in pensive mood,
They flash upon that inward eye
Which is the bliss of solitude;
And then my heart with pleasure fills,
And dances with the daffodils.

by William Wordsworth

We miss our dear friend Sir Toddy
Toddy's friend BooBooBear @BooBooGreen

We miss our dear friend Sir Toddy and his wonderful Valet, Kevin, so much. They are often in our thoughts because we have so many happy memories. Sir Toddy would always be ready to welcome me into the snug at Furry Tails and we would sit and share nightcap. Sometimes a wee dram of whisky or sometimes a fabulous hot chocolate with marshmallows.

He would tell me stories and chortle. I loved his chortle. When I close my eyes, I can still hear it. He would call me Boo, old chap. I loved that. He was so very kind to me and my human. I had so many adventures because of Sir Toddy. I was a lion, a wizard, a cowboy, scooby doo, BooBoo Bond, an ice skater, a pirate and of course an aviator.

We had great fun on the narrow boat. Sir Toddy was the Admiral of course and Reddy and I were Mutineers teehee. We had lots of giggles and chortles. We miss you Toddy and we miss you Kevin.

From Dee...and Potter Winkles!
@sherfordbear and cbs

My McToddyness, as I used to call him. I knew he was special to me, but I didn't realise how much I loved him, until he stopped answering my messages! On our last text conversation, he said he was feeling sick and had had a long, rough week. His final text on July 20th 2019, was 'I'm sure I will be better soon Dee'.

Then I had the call!   He had died.

It took a while before it really hit me...total disbelief. My heart shattered into a million pieces...I'd never speak to my McToddyness again. I'd never be able to hug him again, or make him fudge! We'd never be silly in the Dinker Patch, or walk in the Dinker wood...he'd never be there for me anymore. To fix my pictures, to sort out my computer problems, to help me prepare for TV or film. My dear, sweet friend of many years, was gone.

A cloud of grief surrounded me, and the world had lost its colour. Nothing seemed much to matter anymore. I lost interest in social media...it was a struggle to make any appearance at all! In fact, I lost interest in many things. But I knew he'd want me to keep going; he would, no matter how he felt, he was always there for everyone, sweet, gentle, kind man that he was.

Now, after a year of grieving, it has lifted & I feel rejuvenated, like he's saying to me…'that's enough grieving Dee, snap out of it. You have bears to make, and they make people happy, so get on with it.'

So, I have. And I found the gift within me to make many Toddy Furrington family members, and created his family tree…for all his followers to have a little bit of him in their homes, forever.

These pictures about sums up my friendship with Kevin, said through the immortal words of my Potter Winkles…

I'll Love you forever. Thank you for being so…YOU.

Do you remember the first time we met? I was sooo excited

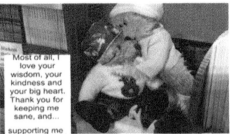

Most of all, I love your wisdom, your kindness and your big heart. Thank you for keeping me sane, and...

supporting me

You chatted with me & I felt an immediate respect; you became my much loved grandpaw who taught me so much.

You let me draw you & write stories about you

You rescued me from Daleks

You've kept me on the straight & narrow!

We walked in the Dinker woods together.

silly old bear

There once was a bear called Toddy
He had clothes made to fit his body
They were smart and well pressed
He was certainly well dressed
And nothing on him was shoddy

Family Tree after Reginald A. Furrington
Created by Dee Dodgson realized by @bearemyted

1.

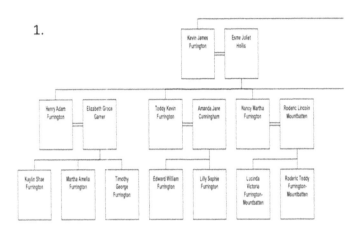

2.

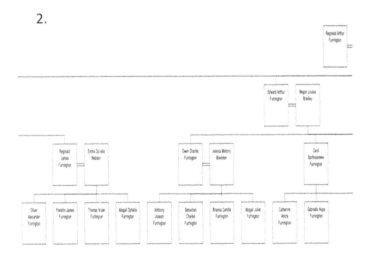

3.

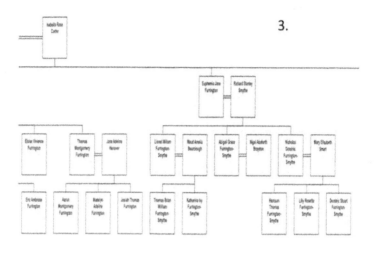

4.

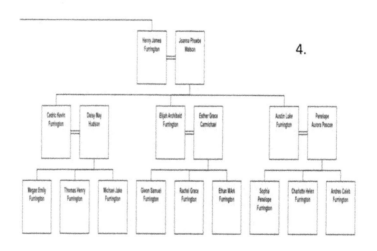

This is an overview of the Furrington family members
Made by Dee Dodgson until September 2020.

The Furrington Family (15)

Photo collage by @belbear

Diesel* @IamDieselBear

Toddy @ToddyFur was one of my first furiends here (Twitter) here, too! I think we can all say that. Me and my people were so fortunate to meet him and his amazing person Kevin in 2017, and their generosity will never leave our hearts.

"Good morning chaps, I hope it's a good start to the week for us all."

Toddy Furrington

The Bear family memories
by Elsie and Chris Bear @belbaer and cbs

We are blessed to have known Kevin in person. When we visited Dee in Plymouth at the end of May this year, we were lucky Dee arranged a personal meeting with Kevin in Exeter.

He came all the long way from Wales (about 3 hours' drive) just to meet us!

What a precious gift!

We waited outside, in a small café near to Exeter Cathedral. We recognized Kevin at the first sight! Why? He was carrying Toddy on his arm when he came across the lawn in front of the Cathedral! We loved him on the first 'hello'!

What a friendly, soft and warm-hearted man!

When he introduced our cousins Ronja and Pru to us, a wool rabbit was sneaking out of his bag. Henry I. he told us, had decided to live with our family! So, Henry became our new family member! He will always remind us to this unforgettable meeting with Kevin in Exeter.

We had so much fun when we walked around this huge cathedral! He surprised us with his immense knowledge about nearly everything!

Our human mum and Kevin had such a good talking

and they felt the same way of thinking like soul mates!

We shared a wonderful afternoon in Exeter and the hours flew away like minutes!

When it came to say goodbye he even bowed himself down to our little hum mum (she is just 150 cm!) and gave her a hug! Mum said to him that she felt honoured that this big man hugged her, the Hobbit! So, our farewell was filled with friendly laughter and waving until he disappeared upstairs to get his car.

He was so young at heart, lively, creative, warm-hearted, helpful, his generosity and giving love to all beings was endless.

He made us laugh and happy by sharing his cubs' adventures with us here and on twitter. His skills in creating perfect sized photo-collages for illustrating #Furrytails adventures, #clubhouse and more with all fine details were amazing!

All these lovely memories will last and will always remind us to our wonderful friend Kevin, the valet of our beloved Headbear Toddy Furrington!

Your helpfulness, faithful friendship, reliability in every sense is your legacy to us. Every day we will try to #BeMoreToddy.

So, you both dear friends, Dr Kevin Phillips and you dear Toddy Furrington will remain being with us. RIP beloved friends! You have departed from this earth, but you'll never truly leave, for you are still alive in our hearts, through us, you live on.

We miss you both each day, every hour, every minute.

Our wounded hearts will heal by the time, but a deep scar will remain.

Farewell dear Kevin and Toddy… someday we will meet again!

Memories of Toddy and his valet Dr Kevin
by Flora Furrington @FFurrington
and Wendy Berry @be75121834

I'd opened my Twitter account in 2013 and for a long-time tweeted photo of places that I visited, my garden and especially my little Jack Russell Terrier Dylan.

From being a small child, I have always loved bears and have quite a Hug and so occasionally I would also post pictures of them as well. I loved to follow bears on Twitter and was delighted that after following Toddy Furrington he followed me back! I loved his tweets, especially his evening tweet when he would say something like he was going to find a cool pillow in the Furry Tails boathouse, you all know the tweets I'm speaking of I'm sure. Toddy was always so kind …

When Dylan passed away in April 2018 and I tweeted my sad news Toddy's reply was beautiful and stays in my mind to this day: "Oh Wendy, I am so very sorry to hear that Dylan has run on ahead OTRB. Our thoughts are with you."

It was so simple really but so expressive and I could picture this and appreciated it very much.

Dylan Berry 2004 - 2018

Another kind tweet came from Toddy at the end of June 2019 when I was with my family and we were out for the day and enjoying a picnic in a park. I tweeted about this and within four minutes, while we were still eating the sandwiches, Toddy replied. I'm sure I could hear his chuckle as he said to enjoy the picnic!

What sadness then when we heard just a few weeks later that Dr Kevin Phillips, Toddy's Valet, had passed away on 7th August.

It is often hard to take it in when someone who has become an online friend passes away. I'm so grateful to other friends who were able to attend the funeral and post photos of the floral tributes ... and also for

the later photos when members of #ToddysHug were taken to say their farewells.
These things are very helpful and much appreciated.

So time went by and, as we all know, members of the Hug went their separate ways. Each was so carefully placed in a new home and I was delighted to welcome little Flora who settled in straight away with WW1 mascot bears Ernest and Fergus and the well-travelled Edmund.

They were so excited to see her and gave her a beautiful hat   A
friendly Canadian bear gave her a cosy top which she wore through the winter.

When we got friended with Gregory Thetmeyer's family @belbaer they sent her a very glamorous red dress and a pretty pink one, too.

Flora is a very happy little bear. She has her own Twitter account @FFurrington so that she can keep in touch with all her friends and whilst life has changed for all of #ToddysHug it is with thanks to @natalie_rizvi, @TourGuideTed, @reddy1408 and @sherfordbear that all of the bears and other pals that lived with Dr Kevin Phillips and dear Toddy have found wonderful new homes and happy new lives.

I am sure that they both look down on us all fondly and are pleased with how things are.

Special thanks to @belbaer for preparing this wonderful book, much love to all, Wendy x

Fred and Ted @FredTedHug

Hello - we didn't write any memories, as we didn't know Toddy but he did serve us at the FurryTails bar when we very first came on to Twitfur. He was so kind and we are thrilled that Auria chose to live with us.

Gecko Communications @GeckoComs

warmest memory of Toddy was his evening sign off...
when he said something like: "Good night everyone,
Its time for this old bear to find a cosy spot in the
#FurryTails boat house. Sleep well" We wish we'd
known him better - it comforted & made us smile
hugs

*"Good afternoon chaps, I'm just arriving at the
#FurryTails bar. How is everyone today?"*

Toddy Furrington

Toddy Furrington @toddyfur on twitter
by Gregory Thetmeyer @belbear

I remember meeting Toddy numerous times at the #Furrytails Clubhouse for sharing a good fresh brew from tap, enjoyed a delicious brunch buffet and more. Chalky and Cuddles were beartastic hosts.

Many friends organized great events and our bartenders were legendary, too. Just to name some: Chalky and Cuddles @chalkybear1965, Archie Steiff @TheHugHouse, Jeremy Bear @jezzerbear ... sorry dear friends, but I am an old forgetful bear.

Toddy and I often had a good laugh about: in case we can't remember of our whereabout, at least we old chaps could make an emergency call to Dr Who!

Our friend Henry @keepfits challenged us in the gym. Toddy once gave us a bearfect @keepfits gym lesson.

Here are Toddy's instructions in his own words with kindly permission by @natalie_rizvi.

In order to the photo collage next page:

01: Hello #keepfits - how are you today? I'll just pop my towel down and get ready to do some gentle warm up stretches on my gym mat
Laying down on my towel at #keepfits and stretching out the old spine... then a little paw wiggling

02: Stretching slowly... one paw up... and relax... the other paw up... and relax...

03: Turn head slowly to the left, and pause and then look to the right... stretch to the left and stretch to the right... warming up slowly

04: Stretching one paw to the left... and relax... and one paw to the right and relax

05: Reaching for the #keepfits gym ceiling... and hold it... and relax

06: Lifting up on my foot paws and stretching... and down... and stretch a leg back.... and relax...

07: "Good night chaps."

Toddy's bearsonal High Fashion tailor, Snuffy N. Bearmani, of "The House of Bearmani" created all of Toddy's exquisite outfits. His Tea hats were made by @HatsPeriod. Here is a small selection:

Rest in peace Toddy's valet

by **Jeremy Bear*** @JezzerBear and cbs
first issued on August 9th, 2019 at:
jezzerbear.wordpress.com

Since hearing the terrible news on Wednesday night of Dr. Kevin's passing, a minute hasn't gone by where I haven't thought of this sad news and shed the occasional tears as well. In fact, I start typing this now through leaky eyes.

I wanted to put down my memories of him so you could all understand what a loss it is to me, and others who he reached out to and the lives he touched, on both social media and indeed in real life. It's true that others on twitter may have known him a little better than me, but simply put, he was a constant in my life since from when I first joined twitter back in 2013. In fact, there are a few constants on twitter for us anipals, those that seek to unite us, those that we rally around and have the comfort of knowing that they are always there for company, advice, or just a bit of fun.

For me these are #FurryTails (previously #TeddyBearEmbassy and #TeddyEmbassy), Zombie Squad, The Aviators, and Henry and friends. There are others too, such as #BTPosse, #NipClub, #TeddyBearScouts, #PalsPorch etc.

I created this blog originally to review chocolates, and I am ashamed to say I have let it lapse for one reason or another. I do remember joking with Toddy once about how lucky I was people were sending me chocolates from around the world to taste and review, and he said perhaps my next one should be reviewing flat screen TVs or Bentleys!

Of course, he was a dab hand at making pictures for pals on twitter (for special occasions, Twitter clubs or just for fun), so I also wanted to share the brilliant, and sometimes hilarious pics he made for me over the many years. He even told me recently which ones his favourites were:

When I first joined Twitter back in January 2013, I must admit my human did it principally as a silly prank to mock my original owner (and mummy), Phillipa, from whom he "borrowed" me. He also wanted to take me on an imminent adventure to Barbados, and tweet those pictures back home to mummy and… well who else? Surely no one else was interested in seeing pictures of a teddy bear on a beach or in a cave or on a boat or interesting building somewhere? Would they?

But suddenly, out of nowhere, I got follows from other teds! Also, adventurers, be it to other sides of the world or just to the end of their beds. Some comforted their chronically ill humans, so well loved that they had little or no fur left after a lifetime of cuddling. Some were on screen avatars for shy or private individuals who wanted to interact with people on social media, but didn't want the minutiae of their private lives shared with every Tom, Dick or Harry. I suspect Toddy fell in that camp.

One of my first friends in those early pioneering days for stuffed toys on Twitter was Toddy, and I was intrigued to be invited to a virtual club he had co-formed with Chalky and Cuddles called Teddy Bear Embassy. Phillipa and I were amused at first, but we soon found it to be a great place to virtually meet up and chat with teds, anipals and honorary humans (as we initially called them) who lived as far afield as Australia, to chat about our adventures or simply just have a laugh.

Eventually, things even got to the stage where addresses were swapped for sending each other cards and gifts. Year on year, my Christmas card list gets longer and longer, and it gives me great joy to send cards around the globe every December, especially to friends whose mantel pieces might otherwise be empty (including mine!)

And then, even "tweetups" were arranged! Who could imagine such a thing? The undisputed king of ted tweetups is Tourguide Ted, although my first ever tweetup was with Mumbas Gabig, who sadly left Twitter many years ago. Many people and furs were having meetups since the invention of the internet I'm sure, but nowadays the teddy tweetups can be quite a huge affair.

But one fur who hadn't been to the early tweetups as far as I was aware was Toddy. But that changed later on, and when the opportunity arose to meet Diesel Bear who was coming all the way from Kansas, AND Toddy Furrington at a tweetup at Cadbury World in June 2017, how could I possibly say no?

Jeremy & Toddy Furrington

It was a nerve-wracking occasion because it was to be a very large gathering of twitter friends, some I had met before and some I hadn't. And for a few, it was their first of many subsequent tweetups around the country. I was glad to meet Sir Scamp too, who came all the way from Glasgow to be there.

And on that lovely day, I met the great man himself, Dr Kevin. (I don't want to call him just Kevin, it doesn't sound right). And what a presence he was. Tall, well spoken, every bit the man I imagined he'd be and more. Full of interesting anecdotes, charismatic, a true gentleman. I already knew how smart he was because we were both members of Snuffy Norton's Canbesocial site, a kind of Facebook for anipals with a charming creakiness to it which just adds to the fun. Toddy was a big fan of Canbesocial and posted on there on an almost daily basis. He had a connection with Snuffy, who made him a lovely paw snitched "Bearmarni" wardrobe for nearly all of his hug including many wonderful outfits for Toddy himself, and they were both Bengal cat owners. Kindred spirits separated by the Atlantic Ocean.

Angel Lexie posts a monthly quiz on CBS, a highlight for many of us who join in, and nearly every single month Toddy got 100% correct. Not surprising to those who knew or ever interacted with him.

There's a weekly Brain Teaser on CBS too, and Toddy would ask the cleverest questions accompanied by another of his charming pictures as a clue. There's a weekly Brain Teaser on CBS too, and Toddy would ask the cleverest questions accompanied by another of his charming pictures as a clue. Answers would be DM'd and those who got them correct were dubbed Brain Boxes.

Anyone who knows me knows I can be a cheeky bear, and sometimes emotional too. Toddy had little patience for my rare emotional outbursts, and I must admit we did fall out a couple of times over the years. But all was forgiven and forgotten and we settled into a happy groove over the final years, with me being careful to show him the respect he deserved. As he once wisely said" No one knows what's going on in a chap's private life".

@TheAviatorsClub · · · #TheAviators

AVIATOR LICENSE

Name: @JezzerBear

Aviator name: Juliet Bravo India 658

Level: A. Aviator

Date: February 1st, 2014   Signature @TheAviatorsClub:

Don't forget to put #TheAviators in your tweets!!!

This is meant for Anipals with a Twitter-account. It has nothing to do with flying in real life.

@JezzerBear on Aviators Adventures

I wish I had gone on more Aviators adventures, or just popped into the Furry Tails bar more often to say hello. But all those wishes won't bring him back. One of the last conversations I had with him was about my lavender plants which were about to go into full bloom. I wanted to show him a picture of the many varieties of bees and insects that are enjoying the flowers, but alas I just never got around to it. This morning I made a small donation to the Bumblebee Conservation Trust in his memory.

So many things I haven't even told you yet. Like how generous he was when donating to charities, or how he was a great supporter of small enterprise such as Kirby Bears, CBS and Dinker bears. Dee, the creator of Dinkers and Twecckles , has even immortalised Toddy in a Twecckle short story, one of a series, available on Amazon.

She and Biddy BT's mum probably knew Dr. Keven better than anyone on Twitter. Or those lovely early days when he'd regale us with his stories of travelling around the world, or the gripping story of the mythical "crocasaurus". I think I've left out a lot actually, but I'll stop now. I just hope he's up there somewhere looking down on us, perhaps at the rainbow bridge, and knows how much he meant to us. Rest in peace dear friend. A toast to you Dr Kevin, I know you were fond of a whiskey.

Cheers to you in heaven Dr Kevin!

KerDunkedunk* @kerdunkedunk

#ToddysHug has come tah livs wif us. His naym iz Zippy. He ah-wived lass Fwydey but I wuz too sad tah ah-nounss it coz my cat en bestess furiend dide dat saym dey. I wuz so sad dat Zippy gayvs me a big #ToddyHug coz he undastoods dat kinda loss too. We cwide tahgevah. We's ok now

The Toddy Furrington star allows us to remember our friend, but sending Toddy, Kevin & Ginger to Mars 2020 with the NASA & #FurryTails Adventure Centre joint expedition seemed more adventurous.
They loved sci-fi but I do hope there's time to stop for tea! by @KerDunkedunk

TODDY FURRINGTON

Celestial Coordinates:
19h 06m 52.5s 37d 48m 31s

Approximate Lifespan:
10 billion years

G class stars like "TODDY FURRINGTON" appear yellow to yellow white in colour. Our own sun falls into this category, so other such stars present a very good chance of hosting varied planetary systems and potentially complex life like that which evolved on Earth.

Remembering Toddy Furrington and his devoted Valet Kevin

by Toddy's Friend **Moretta** @moretta_moon

I never had the opportunity to meet Tod or Kevin in person but I loved reading the posts from both the Teddy Embassy and later the Riverside Hug.

Each night I would imagine Tod was saying goodnight to me personally as he toddled of to his bunk in the Old boathouse.

The joy he bought into my life with his Aunties and the cubs will stay with me always until the day I cross the Rainbow Bridge and finally shake their paws at the Summerland hug Where I know they both now reside.

I had an uncle…

by Dr Kevin's niece **Natalie Rizvi** @natalie_rizvi

Uncle Kevin was larger than life his personality was as big as he was. He loved to take photos took a camera nearly everywhere with him. He travelled a lot. He teaches people how to work new computer systems. He went all over the world. He was a certified diver and he really enjoyed that. He was the kindest of people.

Dr. Kevin Phillips 1962 - 08.07.2019
and Toddy Furrington

Missing them...

by CBS-friends Popz, Bruizzers, Doc Festus and Mr. Tucker (Furrington)

Dr Kevin and his mate Toddy were always so nice and helpful to everyone on our social media sites. They were smart, kind, and funny. They would always brighten up a gloomy day. We will always miss them.

Mr. Tucker (adopted from Toddy's Hug)
Picture of Dr Kevin and Toddy Furrington

"Paws crossed it's a good day for mum, my friend."

Toddy Furrington

Memories of Dr Kevin and Sir Toddy

by **Radar Asher and family** cbs/@RadarAsher

I never met the man but only knew him through his beloved teddy name Toddy Furrington. My teddies named him Sir Toddy because he was so poshed, and so caring, like a grand uncle.

My brass button bears that hang out on Twitter are Radar and his twin sister Rosie Amelia Bearhart. They both got their Aviator license even though Sir Toddy's rules were only one bear per family could qualify, thanks to one of the female Furrington bears who fought for Rosie to get her own license.

Sir Toddy made many graphic pictures for the furry community including Radar and Rosie to go to the different parties at FurryTails that place on Twitter like: Star Wars, Star Trek, Hogwarts, Halloween, and matching up with planes of our choice for our license photos. He was very talented with those graphics.

Oh one time the twins took the Tardis (of The TV show Doctor Who) to #FurryTails on Twitter after hours on their birthday to raid the kitchen and Sir Toddy never scolded them for it.

As for me the human, my memories are very personal and touching, I, like many, have never met Dr Kevin, didn't even know what he looked like. I only spoke to Toddy his beloved bear.

I've struggled with my budget for many years making ends meet living on a pension. I never asked for money but when a long month would come and no money for groceries Dr Kevin would ask for my PayPal. He only did that twice, when I finally worked out my budget to not run out of money for groceries I was so proud of myself I wanted to tell him, so he'd be proud too, that day was a month after he died, when I remembered that he was gone I broke down and cried for an hour. I am crying while writing this, He will be missed.

When they had the funeral and the Aviator "one man missing" fly by memorial service on Twitter I cried hard, could not see the keys to type out Radar's plane flight, It felt so good to be with others, to cry and talk with others who have been touched by a big man with a big heart and his beloved furry poshed little bear.

Sunny Art and Midge
by cbs friend Sunny Art

My dear friend, Toddy. I love you. But every time I think of something to write for the book about you, I draw a blank. I've experienced so much loss that, even though I could talk for days about everyone I've lost, every time I try to focus on that thought, I blank out. I can only say that, if I were to write anything, I would write that you were a wonderful friend to me and to Midge and to everyone lucky enough to know you and your human. Love to you, my friend.

A question sent to Toddy;

"Dear, wise Toddy, I've hit a little problem with a customer…"
Toddy's answer;
"Take a deep breath, thank the person concerned, then leave it. Don't engage with the 'crazies'…deep breath."

Toddy Furrington

"Happy to help with the laptop advice, if I can be of any help."

Toddy Furrington

How I Met Toddy Furrington
by **Ted Bearemy** @BearemyTed

After I discovered Stuffie Twitter and got my own account in April 2019, I started my first tweet attempts. After a short time, Toddy noticed me and immediately invited me to #FurryTails, where I gradually made more and more great furry friends. For me, Toddy was a teacher, friend and somehow a role model for how to behave and move in the virtual place Bearington.

When I heard about Kevin's death I was on vacation and although I had never met Kevin and Toddy personally, I was deeply touched by his death. I could never imagine that I felt so much friendship for someone who was actually a stranger. On the day of his funeral, I could not work smartly all day and if I had somehow been able to I would have gone to England for his funeral.

I have already seen how nice the people behind the stuffed animals are on tweetups in Belgium and London. Also, the people who knew Kevin personally convinced me more and more that Toddy and Kevin was a central institution for the community that is now lost forever.

I have a big goal that I want to achieve by 2021 at the latest. We, the bears from my shared apartment, want to visit Kevin and Toddy's grave-side and pay him the honor he deserves.

They live on in our souls and will not be forgotten. The hashtag #BeMoreToddy says so much and ensures that we will never forget them. I especially miss his almost daily evening greeting when Toddy has retired to sleep in the FurryTails boathouse.
Ted Bearemy @bearemyted

Thomas Montgomery Furrington welcomed by Tumbler at Ted Bearemy's family

From top left to bottom right page 81:

"I have my passport ready – just in case!"

"Uncle invited me to share the Royal Box with him while we watched the Border Terriers Christmas Concert on Twitter. It was such jolly good fun!"

"Showing my tea cupboard."

"I do hope you have had a smashing Christmas and found joy in this season. This time of year, can be difficult for many chaps, so perhaps you might go out of your way to say hello to an elderly neighbour?"

"This cute #Dinker painted box and a ghostly white Poddlewink called Casper arrived from Deedee today. Aren't they cool?"

Oh, very good choices Oscar... I love a shepherd's pie! #FurryTails

In centre: Toddy at #FurryTails clubhouse

Toddy Furrington

teddy tedaloo's toddy and doctor kevin story*
by Teddy Tedaloo @TeddyTedaloo and cbs

i can't be sure how many yearz i was matedz with toddy, but itz been a lot of yearz! we first met on facebook and twitter. he then became real active at the eggcellent bear-and-animal-friendly social networking site canbesocial, run by snuffedy norton. toddy became a regular fixture there and was on every day, and he also stopped in at twitter. heck, i can't remember a day that didn't have toddy in it!

the stuffie/fluffy and animal/anipal communityz could alwayz count on toddy to cheer us up with a famous toddy chortle. he liked to make us smile and offer encouragement. he managed to find something good to say even when there was nuthin good to say! when he liked something, he would say it was "jolly good" or "smashing!" if i posted a comment complaining about mama's cooking, he would be a gentlebear and defend her, saying he was sure mama was a smashing cook! tee hee! if he only knew!

one of my favorite thingz he did was call everybody "chaps." it didn't matter if you were a bloke or a lady— to toddy, everybody was a chap! he even once referred to mama as a chap! i thought it was cool beanz and just a part of his unique toddy style. and boy did toddy have style! he was one of the sharpest dressed bearz I ever knew!

i sure wish i could have met him and his valet/typist, doctor kevin, in person. they lived in wales in the united kingdom. well, i been to wales tonz of times, but i didn't know them back then. to think that our pawz might have crossed paths—or maybe they did cross paths and i never even knew! but it was yearz later when toddy came into my life.

when i produced my 2017 teddy tedaloo calendar, toddy was one of my very first customerz who ordered a copy. though i have a feeling it was really doctor kevin who paid for it. us bearz are sure good at getting our humanz to cough up the cash, tee hee! i still have their email from 11 november, 2016 in my inbox. *kryz*

i wish we could turn back the clock and have toddy and doctor kevin with us again, but I know thatz impossible. so we got to do our best to keep them alive with our memories and remember their kindness and sense of fun. no matter how bad thingz get, we need to #bemoretoddy. because thatz what toddy and doctor kevin would have wanted. yah, they were good matedz to us all!

teddy tedaloo
website: https://teddytedaloo.com
twitter: https://twitter.com/TeddyTedaloo

Tour Guide Teds aka TGT memories

by secretary human Di Gorton
CanBeSocial/Twitter @TourGuideTed

Who would have thought in those early days of the #TeddyBearEmbassy we would now have so many Twitter friends? Or that we'd have met so many.

I met Toddy and Dr Kevin on many occasions, though he didn't make the last one, just last Sunday – he was so looking forward to it this year after work prevented him from coming last year. We shared a love of travel, of train (especially the steam ones), of tea and beer and our love of fun. We got up to so many adventures on Twitter and will continue to take Toddy on my adventures as part of the #Flatties.
The human is leaking again here – so much emotion for a small hug of teddy bears and their larger than life valet.

Rest in peace Kevin – you touched so many lives and will be missed but never forgotten.

We felt the light dim when we heard of the passing of Dr Kevin, valet to our beloved friend Toddy-Aviator, barman, movie buff, Photoshop whizz & more.

We chose to name a star[2] Toddy Furrington for all of us, knowing we can look up & remember our friends Toddy & Kevin

---

[2] photo on page 70

TGT on tweetups
by Di Gorton secretary of TGT

Dippy, The Dinosaur, Birmingham 14 Aug 2018

We had a tweetup in Birmingham to meet Dippy the Dinosaur (a model of a Diplodocus dinosaur skeleton).

Treacle Bear (@Treacle_bear), Kenny Koala (@kennykoalabear), Frank (@TourGuideTed), Sheila Koala (@kennykoalabear), TGT, Otter (Tabitha's Ikkle Human), Tabitha (@TabithaTeddy), Toddy & Ginger (@ToddyFur), Perky Penguin (@perky_penguin), Chomper (@Chomper_TC), Ed, his mate, Jake Squires (@Emergency_Teds), Junior Stanton (Facebook) and Clyde (@littlemore20)

We had timed tickets to meet Dippy

After our tour, we headed to the Edwardian Tea
Rooms in the Museum.

Frank (in the dinosaur head) was having fun
terrorising everyone while we were waiting for tea
and cakes...

The "funny" story part:

When we arrived at the table, as usual all the stuffies piled into the table.

What we didn't immediately notice was the bottle of balsamic vinegar on the table. Shortly afterwards we noticed that a few others had brown soggy wet patches on their fur but worst hit was light-colored Ed who had a very wet bum. Ed doesn't belong to Chomper but is a friend that Chomper gets to take out so Ed can have a little excitement – this was a little too much excitement and now it's even harder to get permission to take Ed out for tweetups! Forever after this incident has been remembered as #BalsamicGate.

Weston Super Mare – 11 May 2018

Ker'D (@KerDunkedunk) and his pals and his human Mah Lisa were over staying with us in England. We decided to go to Weston-Super-Mare one of the nearest beaches to us and a famous British holiday resort (at least it was in the 60s/70s more than now, but it's still a popular resort, but very tacky – donkey rides, amusements, ice cream, pier with an arcade, etc.). Still as it was not far away from Toddy and Kevin we invited them along for the day. Kevin actually booked a day off work to join us! Debbie Kynaston (only on Facebook), then on Twitter as @LUCKYBLUEYHONEY) came with us with her bears Lucky, Bluey and Honey.

We met a tea rooms close to the "Front" (sea front/beach) as this was Toddy so we knew he'd

need tea and bears always need an afternoon tea –
even in the morning! Haha!
After tea, we headed over to the Pier for some fun –
the weather was awful!

photo of Dr Kevin by Lisa

There was a giant deckchair for us to sit in. Not sure Toddy knew what he was getting into but we know how to have fun!

We also rode Thomas The Tank Engine of this!

We took a ride in Winnie The Pooh's honeypot – it went up and down and around

Memories from a day on the Flying Scotsman and Tornado steam trains in

Kidderminster in 2017

Frank (TGT) at the back, Rosie, Toddy, Spy and Q in front, TGT, Pink Ted and Reddy, Junior Stanton (in Stratford hoodie) and Theo (TGT) at the right -photo taken in the café before we set off-

We met up from Wales, Kent, Essex, Lancashire, Warwickshire and West Midlands near me in the Midlands. It was a horrible wet day but this was after the Flying Scotsman had been returned to mainline use. It was a big deal and tickets were hard to get. Still we had a brilliant day out riding the trains and getting photos.

On one occasion we were riding steam trains and at the end of the day, we bears were invited onto the footplate. Assistant D climbed (struggled) on board with us bears and sat us down in front of the firebox, except -of course- a footplate is a bit sooty and covered in coal dust. We all laughed as we got off as we all had sooty patches, particularly Toddy who'd got soot on his fancy Bearmani overcoat.

Spybears: Friend of Toddy @spyteamHQ

Kevin was so kind to Sec that day and she treasures the really interesting chat they had.
Memory of a day out on "The Flying Scotsman".

"Make sure you're not left behind chaps."

Toddy Furrington

Dr. Kevin & Toddy - sharing our memories

by **The Teddy*** on CanBeSocial/ @TeddysFamiwy

The Teddy wasn't too sure what to expect when she firs joined twitter. Being so new to the site, I didnt weawwy think anything would come of me joining. Thare were so many teddys and anipals alweady, the Teddy was sure she would jus get dwowned out and then eventuwy jus stop getting on altogether.

But that was before I met Toddy. Toddy was one of the Teddys vewy firs fwiends on social media. And after meeting him, the Teddy began making more and more fwiends. It was yike a wipple effect and at the vewy center of it, dipping his paw in the water, was   Toddy.

Thare was something vewy speshul about Toddy. We all know this to be twue. A wiser, kinder teddy would be incwedibwy hard to find. The Teddy can't even begin to descwibe jus how vewy happy she is to have known him.

As I have said before, the Teddy didnt know Toddy as well as so many of you. But you all understand that you didnt have to know him long for him to make such a stwong impwession on your life.

Toddy bwought a wot of fun and happiness to us on twitter. And then Toddy intwoduced the Teddy to CBS!

And here Teddy had even more fun wif some new fwiends! I cant bewieve just how many fwiends I have because of Toddy.

Our fwiend Toddy Fuwwington (or wather his valet, Kevin)

The Teddy didnt know Toddy as wong as many of her fwiends did. But he was one of the first fwiends that I made on twitter. And what a fwiend he was! Always so vewy kind and fwiendwy to evwyone, Toddy accepted all newcomers with open arms. He always tweated evwyone wif such wespect and decency. A twuer gentlebear you could not find.

The Teddy wemembers how Toddy would always be wight thare at the #FurryTails bar to offer evwyone a dwink or something to eat! It was always so gweat to go and chat wif him or any other fwiends who were thare. Its gonna take a wot of getting used to not having him thare now.

My little brother Sigh asked me to share something from him too. Toddy was instrumental in him opening #SighsShop. His shop has become pretty popular and Sigh says he has Toddy to thank for that. Toddy would stop by every time Sigh opened his shop.

My bwother Sigh wemembers Toddy well too. He would yike to say something now.

Sigh: Im v-v-vewy sad to hear the n-news about M-mi-mister Toddy. He w-was so nice to m-m-me always!

Sigh: I wememb-ber when I first th-thought of opening m-my shop on twitter. I w-wa-was weawwy nervous at f-f-first but M-mister Toddy encouw-waged me to do it. And Im so g-gwad I did!

Sigh: I d-dont get to open as often a-as I would wi-wike too, but evwy t-time I did open Mister Toddy would always stop by for s-s-some of his favwite sweets! He w-woved his m-m-mint humbugs!! Ill m-miss him stopping by whene-ever I open #SighsShop.

We all have our own memowies of Toddy. The Teddy never got to meet his vawet Kevin but I can onwy imagine what a wonderful person he was.

Im so gwad that some of my fwiends got to meet him. And though the Teddy never got to, Im so so vewy gwad to have met Toddy. Ill never forget the kindness that he bwought to me and to evwyone.

Raja: Hello everyone! I want to say thank you so very much to Teddy and her hug for taking me in when I needed a home. I came from a wonderful home with Dr. Kevin and Toddy. And though I do miss them terribly, as well as the rest of the hug, I'm forever grateful to be part of Teddy's family!

I also wemember Toddy inviting me to join #TheAviators! Such a gweat expewience!! The Teddy wemembers when she first got her wicense! I was so pwoud when Toddy gave it to me!!

THEAVIATORS
Flying License

Name: @TeddysFamiwy

Call: X-ray Tango 28

Level: A1

Date: August 12th 2018

Toddy Furrington
Signed for: @TheAviatorsClub

Thank you, Toddy. Thank you, all of the happiness, you bwought us all here. You will never be forgotten. And you better bewieve that you will always be woved. And will shall all do our vewy best be #BeMoreToddy

The Teddy has jus one more thing to say:

Goodnight Toddy. May you find the most comfortable bed in the #FurryTails boat house. We wove you my fwiend, and we will never forget you.

"Good evening, come on in out of the rain, it's cosy at the #FurryTails bar."

Toddy Furrington

Toddy Furrington

<u>Toddy's comments to the pictures page 109:</u>

I hope we all have a jolly New Year and 2014 is kind to us, each and every one.

A jolly happy New Year my furends. I wouldn't have missed this year with you all. Thank you.

I wish you a Merry Christmas and hope you all have a wonderful time. This year we decided to donate money to an animal shelter rather than give card companies the cash. I hope you don't mind.

My favourite decoration is the tree... I love the smell and everything about it. Ho, ho, ho...

I am jolly fond of Christmas trees… my tree is a real one, but some chap has sprinkled sparkles on it.

I have been a jolly old bear. I was talking with a dear friend about Christmas markets and found myself spirited away explore one. Lots of handmade confections and wooden toys and sausages! A wonderful time!

Some words of conclusion
by Bärbel Thetmeyer, compilation author

Dr Kevin Phillips was an incredible man! How should you describe a person whose personality was so special?
Words fail me, but I'll try anyway.

Favoured by unbelievable coincidences, I was able to meet this great man, in every respect, in person. That was in Exeter / UK in June 2019.

I recognized him from afar, although I had never seen him before. Holding his alter ego Toddy Furrington in his arms, he strode across the large lawn in front of Exeter Cathedral.

He had this charisma that EVERYTHING he did was natural and self-evident.
I felt as much in the here and now as I never felt before.

It was only after his sudden death two months later that I gradually became aware that I had had an extraordinary man as a friend for a long time.
The mourning for him continues unabated not only with me but with all friends.

By summarizing the memories of many friends, I became aware of what, and how much, he did selflessly for others!

He loved ALL people, animals, plants, etc. Nothing was too small for him that he would not have noticed and protected it.

Without many questions, he immediately had the right words and actions for everyone to help.

Help from him was by no means always material. He always found the right way to communicate, also to help the friend to see how he could help himself.

The memories compiled here speak for themselves.

In conclusion, I can only say something that I have never said before about a person:

Dr Kevin Phillips was an 'angel' in the shape of a human being. He lived with us without leading, but always walking by our side, for too short a time!

He left us a huge gift: to recognize in his life a hope for a more humane togetherness
and to live it every day!

"Good night friend. Remember you are loved."

Toddy Furrington

In loving memory of Dr Kevin and Toddy
In 2020, on August 7,
The Angels looked from heaven.
They searched for miles afar,
And deep within the distance
They could see a shining star.

They knew that very instant
This star was theirs to gain,
So they took you up to heaven,
Forever to remain.

Look down on us from heaven.
Keep us free from hurt and pain.
You'll always be within our hearts
Until we meet again.
by @belbear

We're missing someone - so special to us - each
day -every day -all the time.

"Good night everyone, it's time for this old bear to find a cosy spot in the #FurryTails boat house. Sleep well!"

Toddy's famous 'Good Night'!